Selected Poems of Sŏ Chŏngju

MODERN ASIAN LITERATURE SERIES

Selected Poems of
SŎ CHŎNGJU

Translated and with an Introduction by

D A V I D   R .   M c C A N N

COLUMBIA UNIVERSITY PRESS   *New York*

The publisher would like to thank Munhak Chongshin-sa Publishers
for assistance in the preparation of this volume.

COLUMBIA UNIVERSITY PRESS
NEW YORK   GUILDFORD, SURREY
Copyright © 1989 Columbia University Press

PL
991.74
.C5
A26
1989

Library of Congress Cataloging-in-Publication Data

Sŏ, Chŏng-ju, 1915–
  [Poems. English. Selections]
  Selected poems of Sŏ Chŏngju /
translated and with an introduction by David R. McCann.
      p.   cm. — (Modern Asian literature series)
  ISBN 0-231-06794-1
  1. Sŏ, Chŏng-ju, 1915– —Translations, English.   I. McCann, David
R. (David Richard), 1944–   . II. Title. III. Series.
PL991.74.C5A26 1989
895, 7'13—dc19   88-25738
                                                       CIP

Printed in the United States of America

Book design by Charles Hames

18414253   12-11-90
                                          AU

Contents

Contents

Contents

Acknowledgments

I wish to thank Ted and Renée Weiss, publishers of the *Quarterly Review of Literature,* for their gracious permission to reprint a number of my earlier translations of Sŏ Chŏngju's poems from volume 3 of the *Quarterly Review* New Poetry Series. Six of the translations are reprinted from *The Silence of Love: Twentieth Century Korean Poetry,* edited by Peter H. Lee, copyright © 1980 by The University Press of Hawaii. I am also pleased to acknowledge *Graham House Review, International Poetry Review, Modern Poetry in Translation, New Letters,* and *Wood Ibis* for translations, and *Korean Culture* for earlier publication of the essay which became the Introduction. The translation of this collection was assisted by the Korean Culture and Arts Foundation.

The numbers in brackets immediately following the translations are page numbers of the original poems in *Midang Sŏ Chŏngju sijŏnjip* (The Complete Poems of Midang [the author's pen name] Sŏ Chŏngju), published by Minumsa, Seoul, in 1983.

Introduction

BIOGRAPHICAL NOTE

Sŏ Chŏngju, acknowledged to be one of Korea's preeminent twentieth-century poets, was born in Sonun village, North Chŏlla Province, on May 16, 1915. In 1929 he moved to Seoul and entered high school, but was expelled a year later, accused of being one of the leaders of the Kwangju student protests against Japanese colonial rule. Sŏ entered Chungang Buddhist College in 1935, and had his first collection of poems, *Flower Snake,* published in 1941. During the last years of the Japanese occupation he left Korea for Manchuria, where he was living a wayfarer's life at the time of Korea's liberation in 1945.

He has taught for many years at Tong' Guk University in Seoul, where he is now Professor Emeritus. Following his sixtieth birthday he made a world trip that took him through the Americas, Europe, Africa, the Middle East, and East Asia. He has published nine collections of poetry, several other books of literary history and criticism, and various anthologies. His many honors in Korea include the Free Literature Prize in 1965, the May Sixteenth Memorial Prize in 1961, and the Korean Arts Association Prize in 1966.

THE POETRY

Many readers may be drawn to Sŏ Chŏngju's poems for what they reveal about the poet or the country of Korea. One of the satisfactions to be found in that reading is the confirming sense of the familiar for those who do know Korea, or conversely, the equally gratifying sense of the foreignness of the poems. These reciprocal expectations—of experiencing the strangely familiar, or of meeting in poetry the familiar stranger—can be realized in any poem. Yet in either case, only the reader's preconception of what is foreign is confirmed, and foreignness has in the end little to do with a poem's being Korean; it has more to do with the shape of the poem on the page and the peculiar use of language that in its many aspects identifies itself as poetic.

The pages that follow comprise a sampling of Sŏ Chŏngju's best-known poems, starting with his "Self Portrait," published in his first collection, *Flower Snake*. I retain the hope that, despite the readings offered in this essay, the poems will linger as puzzles, coherent structures of words that do not resolve in the end into yet more pieces of data on or about Korea.

Self Portrait

Father was a serf;
he never came home, even late at night.
The only things standing there were grandmother,
      withered
and pale as the roots of a leek,
and one flowering date tree.
For a month, mother longed for green apricots, even
      one.
By the oil lamp set in the dirt wall's niche
I was mother's boy, with black fingernails.
With my large eyes and thick hair
I am said to take after grandfather on my mother's side
who went off to sea, the story goes, sometime
during the year of reforms, and never returned.
For twenty-three years it is the wind
      that has raised four-fifths of me.
Life has become more and more an embarrassment.
Some read a convict in my eyes,
some an idiot in my mouth,
but I will repent nothing.

On such mornings, at the magnificent dawn,
drops of blood mingle with the dew
of poetry settled on my forehead.
For I have come, tongue hanging out,
panting through sun and shade like a sick dog.

[35]

Published in 1941, "Self Portrait" is one of Sŏ Chŏngju's best-known poems, and especially in Korean literary circles it is viewed as a pioneering work, one in which a direct personal voice speaks for the first time in modern Korean poetry. Yet, as a portrait, the poem approaches its subject by a very rounda-bout route, like a meeting to discuss a marriage prospect. Before meeting the poet, the reader must first encounter the father, a person notable principally for his absence. The grandmother is also there—the father's mother presumably, since in marriage the couple would have gone to the father's natal home. While the father is absent, except by inference occasionally at night, the grandmother is faded, soon herself to be absent, gone on to the next world. The mother, in contrast, is very much present, longing for the sour taste of green apricots because she is preg-nant.

When the poet finally appears, all that the reader glimpses is a kind of snapshot: a mother's boy with black fingernails who resembles his grandfather, an indistinct portrait indeed.

Incomplete as the portrait may be at this point, it becomes abstract and even more difficult to discern in the lines that follow. The entire first half of the poem is needed to present the poet's biological parents and grandparents, but a single line is all that is required to learn that it was the wind that raised him. The idea of life as an embarrassment then seems to summarize what has preceded it while simultaneously establishing the premise demonstrated in the next two lines about what others read in the poet's face. When the poet asserts that he repents nothing, the line in turn, can be read, in turn, as recapitulation, or as a prediction to be tested in the lines that follow.

The phrasing of the next two lines is quite suddenly and noticeably poetic. Impersonal and abstract language replace the concrete, anecdotal conversation about the family album that occupies the first part of the poem. Where the initial appearance of the poet resembled a snapshot, the idea of the photographic process itself can describe as well as anything else the phenomenon now unfolding in the poem: objects are first seen in the light of dawn, and through their immersion in the poetic dew their features are made distinct. What emerges from that process, and most aptly from the contrasting qualities of light and darkness, is the poet.

For the first time in the poem and only at the very end, the poet, the speaker, establishes the terms of the simile: "[I am] panting . . . like a sick dog." Hitherto, the speaker had told of the ancestors who had preceded him or reported what others saw in his features. Only at the end of the poem, as the self-portrait is completed, does the poet instruct the reader in how to perceive him.

Yet even at the end, after all the genealogical details have been presented; after the reports have been filed on what others see in the poet's face; even after the poet has finally revealed himself in his portrait of the poet as a sick dog, he remains as thoroughly hidden as at the beginning. The self portrait reveals next to nothing, in fact, about the poet. It succeeds, rather, in deflecting the reader's attention by a series of comments—"Life has become more and more an embarrassment" or "I will repent nothing"—that seem to suggest the imminent revelation of the poet himself.

Taken as a whole, with its disparate parts functioning in concert to entice the reader to wait for the picture to be developed and at the same time to frustrate the very expectations it engenders, the poem is the perfect poetic self portrait. It is the poem, not the poet, that is revealed at the end. This observation may amount merely to recognizing that the occasion for a poem need not be anything more than the poem itself, or that a poem called "Self Portrait" need not portray anything beyond itself. In the face of the reductionist threat implied by this suggestion, the notion that in some ways all poems are the same poem, one can make useful note, nevertheless, of the distinction between the apparent subject of a poem and the poem's exemplification of its form. One might say that the form of the poem "Self Portrait" is like a pitcher into which are poured just as many memories and reflections as are required to fill it. In this conception of poetry, reading a poem becomes a process of working through the form toward the content; and it suggests that in some way the subject matter is hidden by that form, or embedded within it. The search for the meaning in the content sifts through the poem for biographical, historical or cultural information, examples of simile or metaphor, or unusual ("poetic") language. The objective of the search is to demonstrate either similarity or difference; it matters little which it is.

Quite another conception of poetry would say that the form of the poem is integral to or indeed the major objective of the whole enterprise, and that content-as-subject-matter is no more than the raw material out of which the poem, as object, is shaped.

To note the form/content dichotomy at this point is only to acknowledge, although indirectly, that in reading (and translating) poetry we are engaged in searching out and articulating its meaning. Because meaning is apprehended either through or as content, the area of tension between poetic form and content seems an apt one in which to explore a few additional examples of Sŏ Chŏngju's poetry. This is so precisely for the reason that of all the constituent features and characteristics of poetry, form and content do remain discernible in translation.

Introduction

Like "Self Portrait," many of Sŏ Chŏngju's most characteristic poems, those which appear in the anthologies of modern Korean poetry, make use of the counterpoint between the subject of the poem and the poem as subject. They begin by seeming to promise to reveal certain intimate details of the poet's life or memory; they engage the reader with that promise, and then through a series of oblique statements and further details draw the reader in and then past the speaker. They work by a kind of literary jujitsu, deflecting the reader's attack by their mixture of artful reticence and down-to-earth candor.

There is a playful character to the poems that exemplify this attitude, as in the title poem from Sŏ Chŏngju's fifth collection, *Winter Sky.*

> ### Winter Sky
>
> With a thousand nights' dream
> I have rinsed clear the gentle brow
> of my heart's love,
> to transplant it
> into the heavens.
> A fierce bird
> knows, and in mimicry
> arcs through the midwinter sky.
>
> [156]

The poem employs the same kind of precise but abstract detail as "Self Portrait": compare the first two lines of "Winter Sky" with "For twenty-three years it is the wind that has raised four-fifths of me." It ends like "Self Portrait" with an animal following an invisible but somehow determinate path through the natural elements. The two poems employ the same juxtaposition of the self-consciously poetic and the ironic: the lofty tones of "the dew of poetry" and the first five lines of "Winter Sky" are disrupted by the images of the panting, sick dog or the bird's mimicry. The dog and the bird seem to mock the poeticalness of the lines immediately preceding, and yet it may be suggested that it is the dog which makes the one both a poem and a self portrait, while it is the bird's imagined mimicry in the other that demonstrates precisely what a poem is: by its representation of the high seriousness of poetic art and the self-mocking turn from that height of seriousness, the poem itself is enabled to take flight.

A further example, a poem so well known in Korea that its canonization in high-school textbooks serves as the occasion for yet another of Sŏ Chŏngju's poems, will show how Sŏ uses a contrapuntal technique to make a poem seem intimately personal while at the same time concerned about nothing more than itself:

Beside a Chrysanthemum

To bring one chrysanthemum
to flower, the cuckoo has cried
since spring.

To bring one chrysanthemum to bloom,
thunder has rolled
through the black clouds.

Flower, like my sister returning
from distant, youthful byways
of throat-tight longing
to stand by the mirror:

for your yellow petals to open,
last night such a frost fell,
and I did not sleep.

[93]

Introduction

The first two stanzas of "Beside a Chrysanthemum" state the temporal relationship between the flower's blooming and some other event, the cuckoo crying or the thunder rolling. What is logically only a temporal relationship, however, is stated in both stanzas as causal, almost genealogical. The reader may also note the silence of the flower's blooming and the noise of the cuckoo or the thunder: from sounds, silence.

The third stanza articulates a relationship between the flower and a sister, a relationship that simultaneously encompasses the past and present, the human and natural, the felt or remembered and the observed, all in a single sentence that is almost too complex to be articulated with the available structures of normal grammar: a sentence sufficiently complex, at any rate, to have given this translator pause more than once. The sentence proceeds verblessly from one phrase into the next like a set of nesting boxes, until by the midway point, at the colon that marks off the long apostrophe to the flower, the yellow chrysanthemum has become suffused if not supplanted by the remembered image of the sister, and not as she is now but as she was at a time so long ago it makes the throat ache just to think of it. Now it is for *that* flower, which is both past and present, human and botanical, that frost fell, and the poet, in a phrase redolent of the attention required either to write or read the poem, did not sleep.

The whole poem acts in effect as a conditional clause for that last statement, "I did not sleep," and that statement in turn answers the question implied by the title of the poem: Beside the flower, what? What happened? The answer is not merely that a poet did not sleep. I suggest that the final phrase conveys something of the attentiveness required by the poem, or any poem. Another way of connecting these points is to ask what does happen between the title of the poem and the final line. The answer: a poem opens up like a flower.

The yoking of structurally opposed elements is a characteristic feature of Sŏ Chŏngju's poetic practice. If a temporal setting is established in the first part of a poem, another time then intrudes. If a natural object is presented, a human element will then be substituted or superimposed. And if language is recognizably poetic in one passage, one can anticipate in the next section of the poem the intrusion of the earthy, the ironic, the aggressively plain.

The juxtaposition of disparate elements in Sŏ Chŏngju's poetry, such as contrasting styles of language or the human and the natural, centers so strongly at times upon other worlds and places that it becomes a kind of subtheme or leitmotif. Indeed, starting with his earliest poems and continuing to his most recent, Sŏ Chŏngju has shown a powerful fascination with the other world, or with other worlds. That world may be the world of memory. It may be the Buddhist world, particularly as represented by the Silla Kingdom (seventh to tenth centuries), a period of official ascendancy of the Buddhist religion. It may just as likely turn out to be the wanderer's world, as in the collection *Wanderer's Poems* (1976) recounting the poet's travels around Korea at the time of his sixtieth birthday, or *Like the Moon Going Westward*, the collection recording his round-the-world journey in 1977 and 1978. In all of these settings, the poems show the interpenetration, juxtaposition, or superimposing of one time or place by, with, or upon another.

Snow Days

Long, long ago my love fell asleep,
perhaps a thousand years before.

Wherever she is sleeping,
she sends me only the colors of her dreams.

Pink, soft pink
azalea hues of her spring dreams.

> Red, deep red, the elm tree's red
> in the murmuring hues of her summer dreams.
>
> And now that snow is falling,
> falling, and piling deep,
> we are apart.
>
> Woman resting by my side:
> in the crescent moon that rises toward your finger's tip,
> again my love's dream shines.
>
> [166]

In "Snow Days" (from *Winter Sky*, 1968), two women occupy the space of the poem. One is the poet's absent love of a thousand years ago and the other the woman resting by his side. It is a lovely but odd poem, anachronistic in a lively and literal, as well as literary, sense. The poet sees the hues of his love's dreams in the pink or red colors of spring azaleas and the summer elm, but in the whiteness of winter he can find no trace of her; no trace, that is, until he notices the pink crescent at the base of the fingernail of the woman resting beside him.

Despite the difference in subject matter, the structure of "Snow Days" bears such a close resemblance to "Self Portrait" that note should be made of it. The first section in each poem establishes its historical origins, presenting the actual progenitors or the historical—mythical—ancestral love. The next section describes in each case what the genealogical or historical forebears have transmitted to the present, the aspects of physical appearance in "Self Portrait" or the dream colors in "Snow Days." The magnificent dawn in "Self Portrait" and the falling snow in "Snow Days" then establish a natural, visual ground on which the final apparition manifests itself. The falling snow first obliterates the connection between the past love and the present moment, just as the wind had obscured while seeming to explain the connection between the poet's progenitors and his present dog-like humanity. And just where the dog–poet emerges from the sun and shade in "Self Portrait," the love's dream, the source of illumination at the center of the poem, shines again on the small viewing screen at the close of "Snow Days."

A final example of Sŏ Chŏngju's use of temporal and spatial juxtaposition is taken from *Wanderer's Poems:*

Snowy Night

On Cheju Island where I spent
Christmas night my sixtieth year
wandering about
and met that girl in the wine house
by the shore—
she had learned my poem
"Beside a Chrysanthemum"
from her high-school language book
and still could recite it perfectly.
When some pesky drinking friend said
"Here, come meet the writer,"
she drew to my side and hid
her eyes in the folds of my coat,
sobbing—that child:
Is she crying somewhere as the snow falls this night?
Or have her tears dried? Has she learned to laugh out
     loud?

[372]

Ostensibly no more than an idle note, "Snowy Night" concerns itself with the juxtaposition of generations and the learning that connects them. The poem has the odd effect of making

Sŏ Chŏngju his own ancestor when the poem "Beside a Chrysanthemum" is handed down to him as part of the wine-house girl's conversational entertainment.

Recollecting the earlier poem as any Korean reader would—a Korean reader would, indeed, be challenged to do so, since the poem is included in high-school textbooks—the reader may discover in the wine-house girl a figure reminiscent of the sister in "Beside a Chrysanthemum." In place of the previous poem's "throat-tight longing" for an even earlier time of "youthful byways," in "Snowy Night" the wine-house girl felt like crying, and may now feel like laughing. In the artificial gaiety of the wine house and the poem performance within it, she may have wept when the fragility of that world was made apparent by the entrance of the writer. When the poet enters, and by his identity as author of the poem reconstructs the terms of the girl's world in the wine house, where she had briefly made the poem hers by reciting it, the effect is literally shattering.

The recitation was part of the girl's performance, an effort to be attractive and entertaining. However, in the poet's retelling of it, the performance turns her from a wine-house girl into a child, rather than into a wine-house woman; it reasserts the generational distance between the author of the poem and the girl who learned it, while at the same time confirming that the sixty-year-old wanderer is the same person as the (famous) author of "Beside a Chrysanthemum."

Through *Like the Moon Going Westward,* the poems from Sŏ Chŏngju's record of his round-the-world journey, the reader will glimpse many of the expected places, buildings, and works of art that appear on any tourist's map.

Often those scenes are presented in ways that connect them to Korean counterparts: the mother and child skating in Ottawa remind Sŏ Chŏngju of a Korean legend; the story associated with Mont Blanc is similar to the poet's "Karma Song"; the floor in Goethe's house resembles the floor of the verandah in grandmother's house; a Swiss watch reminds the poet of Professor Yang and the complicated lecture schedule he followed. Other poems offer more personal observations, sometimes witty, as in "Nevada," rueful, as in "The Pedlar Women of Wu-Lai," or angered, as in "Map of the Arabian Desert."

More than the usual concerns about translation and the poetry that gets lost in the process, I feel a lingering worry about how well these poems will travel back toward the non-Korean setting from which they came. They were written, after all, for a Korean audience anticipating glimpses of the foreign "familiars" of the travel books. How will the non-Korean reader view those same familiar places in a Korean poet's renderings? Will they seem *too* familiar? Or no more than picturesque because of the Korean view they present?

The poems in this last section link places in the Western reader's own landscape with elements of a Korean landscape which the reader of this collection will come to know, and they create through that juxtaposition a new space for our old, familiar friend, the poet Sǒ Chǒngju, to travel through. To borrow another poet's invitation: "You come too."

Selected Poems of Sŏ Chŏngju

Flower Snake   (1941)

Self Portrait

Father was a serf;
he never came home, even late at night.
The only things standing there were grandmother, withered
and pale as the roots of a leek,
and one flowering date tree.
For a month, mother longed for green apricots, even one.
By the oil lamp set in the dirt wall's niche
I was mother's boy, with black fingernails.
With my large eyes and thick hair
I am said to take after grandfather on my mother's side
who went off to sea, the story goes, sometime
during the year of reforms, and never returned.
For twenty-three years it is the wind that has raised four-fifths
    of me.

Life has become more and more an embarrassment.
Some read a convict in my eyes,
some an idiot in my mouth,
but I will repent nothing.

On such mornings, at the magnificent dawn,
drops of blood mingle with the dew
of poetry settled on my forehead.
For I have come, tongue hanging out,
panting through sun and shade like a sick dog.

[35]

Leper

Saddened by the sun
and blue of the sky

the leper ate a child
at moonrise by the barley fields

and through the night cried out
his sorrow red as a flower.

[37]

4

Midday

A path through a field of red flowers
that plucked and tasted bring dreaming death;

along the path winding like the yellow back
of an opium-stunned snake,
my love runs, calling me after,

and I follow, receiving
in my two hands
the blood flowing sharp-scented from my nose.

In the broiling midday, hushed as night,
our two bodies burn.

[38]

Poem of Sudae-dong

Changed into the old, white
cotton clothes—
Now my thoughts lean
by a chill, stone wall,
wrapped in the old ways
that seem remote as Koguryŏ's kingdom.
Eyes closed. The dim
village of my soul returns,
and like stars emerging,
the strange, familiar ways of speech come back.

The lamp had been put out;
my life, long before
gone wrong. And that girl
from Seoul, troubling as Baudelaire,
was forgotten at last.

Number 14 Sudae-dong, in the shadow
of Sonwang Hill: a house built of earth
by the clan head, the old man
who dried salt in the fields
by the Changsu River.
My mother excelled at digging clams.
Father could carry thirty bushels on his back.

Just ten years ago
that girl was with me here,
her hair pinned up,
wearing a green blouse for March.

Not long now. Spring
draws on, and I shall take that girl's
sister, her younger, dark-browed sister,
and live again in Sudae-dong.

[44]

Postcard

TO KIM TONGNI

With my hair cut short
I don't have the face of a poet.
I like the sky; I laugh
through my hard teeth,
and feel pleased as my fingernails
grow thick as tortoise shells.

Let us talk
       of a maiden
              lovely as the cuckoo
when you and I are dead
in the next world.
Why should we seem aristocratic,
like the slim-necked Li Po?

Even on Verlaine's moon-
lit nights, I braid rope
with young Poktong.
If I should still hear the nightingale,
I will cut off my shameful ears.

[48]

Screech-Owl

From what ill temper does he come
each night at midnight to moan out his complaint?
To my father and mother, to me,
even to the one who will be my wife
it is clear he bears some grudge.
My poems, first;
my expression next, down to
each lock of my disheveled hair:
he peers even in daylight
from distant, unmoving shadows,
murmuring some strange incantation.
Heavy, blood-red waves of another world
drench his wings to the roots.
With staring eyes turned to the heavens,
screeching, screeching . . .
screech-owl, you
have built and long inhabited
a round nest in the dark night of my mind.

[50]

The Sea

I listen, but the sea and I are the only ones here.
Above the countless waves drawn in and out,
countless nights come and go,
the road always somewhere,
as the road finally is nowhere.

Now without even a light
the likes of a firefly, in perfect darkness
hide your tear-drenched face. You
sink into the heart
like a single petal
floated upon the sea's mute heart-depths.

Muttering sea, overborne by its own blue
passion, bearing the globed heavens
on its back:
over the sea's depths, young man,
you must blow the four-holed *p'iri.* *

Forget your father,
your mother;
forget brothers and sisters, your family
and friends;
forget at last your woman
and go to Alaska! Arabia!
Go to America! Africa!
Go!
Go, sink down! Sink!

* *p'iri:* a small bamboo reed instrument
having a piercing nasal sound.

Alas, above the weight of a whirling heart,
with hair scattered like leaves,
must my anguish fill the seas?
Open your eyes! Open your loving eyes!
Mountains and sea, North South East
and West, our homeland is drenched in blood and night.

Go to Alaska!
Go to Arabia!
Go away to America!
To Africa!

[55–56]

The Cuckoo   (1948)

Alleyway

Day after day
come out and go
back through this alleyway.

Poor, broken-off
people watching the ground,
coming and going through this alley.

Not sad at all, the blue skies
cover this alley like a thin quilt.
Pale gourd flowers
blooming on roof tops.

Desolation
floods every nook.
When the wind blows
this alleyway shakes
as if in an instant
it might blow away.
Life in a hut,
or this alley, where P'alman
the beggar and Poktong live.
I will cherish the alley
until I grow old,
and I will live in this alley
until I die.

[68]

Blue Days

Dazzling blue days—
Know the longing for those we love.

The green in autumn's garden
withers to autumn hues;

snow fall
lets spring return.

And if I should die and you live?
Or you die? And I live?

On dazzling blue days we know
the longing for those we love.

[73]

Selected Poems of Sŏ Chŏngju   (1956)

Looking at Mount Peerless

Poverty is no more than the tatters, rags
that cannot hide our flesh,
our hearts like green ridges
bared to the brilliant, summer sun.

Like these green hills that raise
orchids on their knees,
we shall raise our young.
Now in the afternoon you shall
turn aside to rest.
Seated, at times,
and at times lying side by side,
wives shall gaze up at husbands
who soothe their brows.

Abandoned, lost in thickets
of brier, we shall know that we are
emeralds, hidden deep under moss.

[90]

Beside a Chrysanthemum

To bring one chrysanthemum
to flower, the cuckoo has cried
since spring.

To bring one chrysanthemum to bloom,
thunder has rolled
through the black clouds.

Flower, like my sister returning
from distant, youthful byways
of throat-tight longing
to stand by the mirror:

for your yellow petals to open,
last night such a frost fell,
and I did not sleep.

[93]

My Poems

Springtime, long ago. With a lady related to me I had entered the shade of a camellia tree growing within the village walls. The lady was seated as if she simply knew which part of the sky it was that had brought those splendid flowers into bloom, while I gathered up the blossoms that had fallen all around us and placed them in the folds of her dress. I kept on repeating that act, without stopping.

For years since then I have been writing poems that tell of my feelings, all like my feelings as I gathered the flowers for her.

But now for some reason there seems to be no one on this earth to give them to. The flowers that I have gathered to give away have fallen from my hands and tumbled across the ground, and there is no other way to write my poems.

[100]

Silla Notes   (1960)

Waiting

My waiting has ended.
The last one I waited for
now having crossed over the curve
of this date tree,
at last my waiting has come to an end.

The early spring and the bright days of fall,
my dream leaf of this world,
date tree fruited with effect,
I have now pushed on toward the next world.
My waiting has ended.

[127]

Autumn Day's Refrain

Persimmons along the hedge are dyed astringent;
cockscomb hollyhock, red.
How am I dyed this autumn day?

Last year's dipper gourds like big fists lie in the yard;
this year's tiny fists outside.
Where shall I lay my fist?

[143]

Between Two Junipers

Like the sun dangling between two Chinese junipers,
chi-jing, chi-tta-jing,
O heart, make a noise now,
a sound as of silver and gold.

My bride being neither water nor blood,
the last flower-bed evaporated, leaving
a blue-black inner field for the seed.

For destination,
there is no road that draws me
if it is not the way
toward the gold-colored world of the west.

Heart, O heart!
Take the bride of this morning
who has dried up, thin as your own vein of ore,
and with a *chi-jing, chi-tta-jing,*
see if you can make a sound
of silver and gold.

[146]

Karma Song

When was it? I bloomed as a single
peony. And one pretty maid who lived
beside me, the two of us
watching each other's faces.

One day after,
the peony petals fell, dried
to ash, became one
with the earth.
Soon that maiden too,
she died and was buried
in that edge of the earth

where the rains poured down,
down on peony, ashes to earth,
washed away with the river
waters, the blood
of the maiden, stored
under the earth, flows
away with the river.

Ashes, peony ashes
in the river's water
turned into flesh
and blood of the fish,
and currents of the river
joined in their flow by the maiden's blood
surged near that fish,
that fish transported with joy
leaps from the waterfall at the edge
of the sky,
snatched up by a bird,

lifted up into the sunshine,
the maiden following too
into clouds under the bird's wing,
till the bird, struck by the hunter's arrow,
falls, though the cloud would hold it,
drawing the cloud down, the showers
pouring down into the yard
of the house
where the dead bird was carried.

That house, the man
and the woman at table
take and eat the flesh of that bird.
Soon, twin babies are born
to that house,
and the couple raise them,
while the shower that fell in the yard
soaks deep into the seed
of the peony that sprouts and climbs,
again climbing high on the stem of the flower.

This yard, this day the peony bloomed,
maiden and peony again gazing at each other,
and already the maiden
has entered the blossom and the blossom
of yesterday's peony
is what I became,
looking on.

[154–55]

Winter Sky   (1968)

Winter Sky

With a thousand nights' dream
I have rinsed clear the gentle brow
of my heart's love,
to transplant it
into the heavens.
A fierce bird
knows, and in mimicry
arcs through the midwinter sky.

[156]

33

Like a Wind from Lotus Blossoms

Sadly, though not
terribly
      just
a bit
sadly

parting, though not
forever
      parting
as if to meet again
in another life

like a wind away
            not toward
lotus blossoms

not the wind you met
a few days ago, but the wind
of a season or more
past.

[157]

A Flower Blooms

Cool water that rinses
a bowl
      leaves
the empty vessel.

The thinnest cloud
has its parting.

A flower blooms bright
red in sunlight,

is just the shadow
over your eye,
the minute shadow that once
or twice veiled your eye.

[158]

Love Asleep

Love sleeps,
while I
am the crane
flying in the white embroidery
on his pillow side.

The red gemstones in his dream
one by one sink down and settle
in the sea of his dream,

and for each jewel that settles there
I must bear our parting.

The gold ring my love removed
before sleep, that slender
gold ring already encircles
my sky.

Filled with his dream,
to return to the gold-threaded
edge of his pillow,
I must bear
yet one more parting.

[159]

Autumn Night

The line of a brow glimpsed just once
in sunlight suffused with the color
of dates.

Brow that was carried
locked up in a heart
leaving home.

Line of a brow that lived hidden
under twelve knives.
That day the knives,
quite rusted away,
were tossed in a ditch,

the New Year fast day
your brow
was so clear.

Uneasy, pressing
against the rocks
on distant crags:

Moon,
Moon, O Bright Moon!
Moon bright
for Ch'usŏk:

In what back room
did you sit up sleepless,
to draw that brow
down the tiles of the roof?

[164–65]

Snow Days

Long, long ago my love fell asleep,
perhaps a thousand years before.

Wherever she is sleeping,
she sends me only the colors of her dreams.

Pink, soft pink
azalea hues of her spring dreams.

Red, deep red, the elm tree's red
in the murmuring hues of her summer dreams.

And now that snow is falling,
falling, and piling deep,
we are apart.

Woman resting by my side:
in the crescent moon that rises toward your finger's tip,
again my love's dream shines.

[166]

My Love's Fingertip

In the pink of my love's
fingertip
lives the song I have not sung to the end.

As I drew away
leaving that song uncompleted,
above the twilight's serenade
and beyond the sliding door,
the newly rising moon.

Coming back with that moon,
playing the violin,

in the fourth string a melody is hidden
that I cannot recall, however I try.

In the pink of my love's fingertip,
her mother's gentle smile,
on a day of utter stillness
in a previous life,

and still in the pink of my love's
fingertip, one dazzling dream
that through the storm-driven days
of this life
I have dreamed and dreamed
without reaching the end.

[174–75]

Rhododendron

A mountain is reflected
in each petal of the rhododendron.

On the mountain's skirts
a sad concubine's house is napping.

On the porch is set out
a chamber pot of brass.

Beyond the mountain,
shoals of yellow fish in the spring tide

and gulls that cry
at the pain of salt.

[180]

If I Became a Stone

If I became
a stone

stone would become
lotus

lotus,
lake

and if I became
a lake

lake would become
lotus

lotus,
stone.

[184]

In the Old Capital

A boy of fifteen or sixteen carrying a bundle of peonies behind on his bicycle passes the alleyway of the old, Yi Dynasty tiled-roof houses, and he calls out in his rooster voice "Buy some flowers." The pulsing of that sound fills air dyed the most beautiful jade in the world. Behind him, a woman wanting flowers opens the white paper window and calls out "Boy, you boy! Come here!" But he doesn't hear at all and goes on eagerly shouting "Buy some flowers! Buy flowers!" Starting up the hill where the dark tiled-roof houses end, riding briskly ahead of the peonies he goes darting away, ringing his bell.

[187]

Lightly

My beloved, the promise to meet
shall be broken no more
as in play my eyes
wander slightly.
In place of you, to consider
a blade of grass
only lightly,
while in the space between us
building a temple,
establish a temple
leaf my eye wanders lightly to.

[193]

Wanderer's Bouquet

Once one year, and I don't know when,
so lonely I could not stand it,
I became a wanderer and spent the year
roaming the mountain district,
and as I did I broke and gathered
a handful of flowers, a bouquet.
That bouquet of flowers I
gave to some child by the roadside.

That child by the roadside
by now must have grown,
and perhaps being lonely he too
has plucked a handful of flowers
to give to some other child.

And after some tens of years have passed,
crossing over yet one more bridge,
might that present of the bouquet
pass on to a child I haven't seen?

And so on a certain day
one thousand, or one thousand five hundred
years from now, below a mountain
where the sky is clearing after rain,
on a vast plain as the sun begins to fall,
where the hand of a new wanderer extends the bouquet,
is the child coming to receive it?

[211]

44

Collected Works of Sŏ Chŏngju   (1972)

Four A.M.

Someone
has soundlessly
washed away

the smudge
of my fingertips
on this stillness

and in that place
newly opens

an orchid
at day-
break.

[236]

History, Korean History

History, our history. Korean history.
Color of Yi Dynasty porcelain
buried in the earth,
the hue at two in the morning
of that porcelain buried in the earth,
our history, O Korean history!

As the sky clears again after rain,
come out playing the *kayagŭm*,*
come out with Ch'unhyang's† step;
try just once
what it is to be the pomegranate,
the Chŏlla‡ pomegranate.

Getting married, or going as a guest,
once the sun is up, try riding
the palanquin just once.
Following your procession now
I have become the forest wild goose.

History, our history, Korean history!
Wearing the Korean socks
and in a dress of deepest red, come out
and try just once,
pomengranate at the edge
of the buckthorn fence.

[242]

* *kayagŭm:* a zither-like instrument.
† Ch'unhyang: the virtuous heroine of
one of Korea's favorite folktales.
‡ Chŏlla: the southwestern provinces.

Such a Land

Do you know a land
whose people live more still, more forlorn
than a temple deep in the mountains,
the fourth hour past midnight,
a quiet dream?

Do you know of a land whose people live
with their words folded away, hung
on a rack beneath the clothes
worn for occasions?

Whose flesh is cheapest in the world.
A land where a dollar is more than enough
to buy two or three pretty young poppies,
and the heart
is never sold. Perhaps
pawned, but never sold, despite
two thousand years'
betrothal.

And with that pledge redeemed,
starting home, a land
that could live on kimchi,
rice,
and water,
ten thousand years
for another such pledge
to wait.

Where the sun
will return, eyes cast aside
like a remorseful lover—
Do you know of such a land?

[243–44]

My Wife

To keep me from wandering
my wife has set out
on the kitchen terrace
three thousand bowls of water.

My rumpled clothes
and *p'iri* * —the sound of a breath
drawing the scent of cold water,
three thousand bowls.

If she should be first
to let her breath go,
I will obtain it
and pipe the *p'iri* full.

If I should be first to climb
away into the skies, I will pour down
breath into her empty bowl.

[248]

* *P'iri:* a small bamboo reed instrument
having a piercing nasal sound.

Spring Lean

A fortnight hungry, this child
hides his face in a mountain.
Seated on a rock he looks
up at flowers in a too-tall tree;
as if he were seated at a rich table
he laughs.

The child another fortnight hungry
hides his face with two mountains,
hears that news from winds
at the cloud tips, and laughs
as if seated at a table
for two,

while the child
yet another fortnight hungry
hides his face with three mountains,
and whether he heard the news
of that news
or not,
like a child who has eaten
will, gently rises up and goes
away with a weary laugh.

[250]

52

Impressions of Grandmother

Grandmother who wore birchwood shoes from Tan'gun's* time
and her fingernails to make the crane cry . . .
Like mugwort, she was, or garlic, or the millet stalk,
Grandmother who taught breathing at low tide . . .

[258]

* Tan'gun: mythical founder of Korea.

Looking at a Yi Dynasty Rice Bowl

Seeing this plain porcelain bowl

laundry hung on a line
in the corner of my yard . . .

white clothes, trousers and blouse
I shall leave unfolded forever.

Like my brother taken
north during the war,
these clothes strung out
like a brother who will never
return,
I am ready now
to have as they are.

[263]

Last Stone

The one who watches the last stone,
the child is left;

the one who watches that child
remains God the Father.

Crowded out by popcorn peddlars and sandwichmen,
God stays alone, turning aside.

Hanging about kibitzing at someone's *Paduk* * game,
God the Father is left alone.

[276]

* *Paduk:* the game with black and white
stones, known as *Go* in Japanese.

Stories of Chilmajae Village (1975)

Untitled

"Pine flower's blooming," says
a friend on the phone
a hundred miles away.
"Try to imagine the scent."
"I am
        thinking of it," I say
to myself, facing
a thousand years away.
"Can you sense it . . .?"

[275]

The Big Wave

There was a day when the sea overflowed, climbing back up the stream, sliding through gaps in the hemp-stalk hedge, crossing over the corn patch to gather brimming in the yard of my grandmother's house. On that day I would have been visiting for minnows or shrimp fry, and hopping around chirping, happy as a lark. Grandmother, who always seemed able to spin stories out long as the silkworm's thread, this time for some reason was utterly still. She stood, her old face tinged reddish, like twilight, staring mutely out to sea.

I did not understand, that day, but now that she has passed away I have at last begun to. Grandfather was a fisherman, sailing far out to sea, and one autumn, before the time I was born, they say that in a sudden storm he was swept away overboard and forever lost. There was simply nothing grandmother could say, though her face flushed red, when she saw the waters of her husband's sea returning to the yard of his own home.

[281]

Shoes

The shoes my father bought me for holiday wound up being sent off to sea, down on the stream where I was playing. Perhaps those shoes of mine have already passed through the inlet by the nose of Pyŏn Mountain, and in my stead they are wandering now along the shores of this world.

My father bought another pair of shoes in place of those, but they could never be more than substitutes; I had to face the holidays wearing substitutes on my feet.

And now though I am all of sixty and have bought many pairs of shoes, I still have not changed that habit of mine, of buying substitute shoes.

[285]

Grandmother's Verandah

Behind grandmother's house is the verandah, dark as mulberry-wood and big as two sheets of floor paper. Verandah polished each day, it was said, by grandmother's hands and the hands of her daughters, so there must remain many signs of the youthful touch of my own mother's hands. By now though that floor has been polished so often, the marks of so many hands have been worn away to a gleaming mirror, a mirror reflecting my young face.

It happens on a day when mother is so mad, scolding me till I have no place to go, I find this verandah, mirror of time and touch. I catch my breath, and eat the healthful fruit grandmother picks and gives me from the mulberry out by the sauce-crock terrace. Even mother cannot bring her scolding back here, to this verandah where my face and grandmother's are reflected side by side.

[286]

Stone-Woman Hanmul's Sighs

Barren, she found a second wife for her husband herself, Hanmul who lived alone by the pine grove on the hill. Her name was not the name of her village, Han-mul, "Lots of Water"; she was tough and plump and smooth as jade. Eyes and eyebrows, teeth and the whorl of hair: of all the women in Chilmajae Village, Hanmul's were the most clear and shapely. In strength too.

On a windy day as she was passing along the roadway among the cotton plants with a basket of corn on her head, as the cotton plants turned their white bellies in the wind the village people made her laugh as they called "That too is because you're so strong."

On her face always a quiet smile emerging like a flower that bloomed in jade, a smile in difficulty or at ease that would curl the upper lips of man or woman, young or old, till their upper teeth showed. She had that strength. Such a powerful smile, they said, that people could not watch it too long, but would turn their gaze aside. And they say not just people, but dogs and cats as well were affected. It became a saying, "Live and make people laugh like Hanmul."

But that laugh and Hanmul's smile were taken from this world by a fever, when Hanmul was only forty or so. And in the village another story started, that has lived on until this day. They say they hear Hanmul's sigh. It was early, on a clear morning, soon to turn bright, when the morning sun was just starting to climb. Not dark night, nor the usual rainy or cloudy day, but on a day they say when the sun seemed to be gathering itself to leap up, a sound came mixed with the soft breath of the pine groves just a pace or two behind her house.

Now on a bright morning when they hear the sound of wind in the pines, the people say "There it is! Do you hear? Hanmul must have gotten up early. You can hear her happy sigh again. This will be a day for laughter."

[302]

Aloeswood

Those who would make the incense wood immerse pieces thickly cut where the waters of the mountain-valley stream meet the sea. After years and years have passed they remove the pieces, dry and split them and use them for incense.

The wood, they say, must be kept submerged for two or three hundred years; then one can smell the right fragrance. And even better are the pieces submerged for a thousand years.

So it is that the people of Chilmajae take the pieces of aloeswood and send them down into the confluence of earth and seas, not for themselves, nor their own sons and daughters; not for grandsons and granddaughters, but for some future generation too far away to see.

And so the hundreds and thousands of years between the one who puts in and the one who takes out are only the most intense longing, the very fragrance of the scented wood with nothing faint, distant, nothing lonely, nothing that is not extraordinary about it.

[309]

Wanderer's Poems   (1976)

Poetics

The sea women of Cheju
    diving for abalone deep in the sea
leave the very best of the shells they find
    stuck to the rocks deep down
in the water, to pluck and gather
    the day their loves return.
The very best shellfish
    of poems too:
                    Leave them there!
What empty, aimless wandering
    if every last one is gathered up.
Longing for the sea, just leave it there,
    this being a poet.

[328]

Cuckoo's Cry

The sound of the cuckoo's cry
descends, caressing your shoulder,
circles round the tip of your socks,
circles ten times, or twenty times round.

The yellow-gold ring from your wedding day, long ago:
Now kept by a pawnshop,
the gold line of that ring that turns
in your memory, turning, and turning,
the cry that comes sounding . . .

The branch of the black pine
standing at the crossroad,
as the sound passes by, washing
the pine branch that teaches
the way of youth to you
who try on the servant's role.

[330]

New Year's Prayer
1976

The sound of the boy walking
down the snowy street
selling fried silkworms

echoes the rustling of bamboo groves
near Tamyang, in the southwest.

Sharing a grin with him I know
a difficult calm.

The boy selling papers,
as he pulls a copy loose from the pile,

the sound of pine groves
near Ch'ongdo, east of Taegu.

Placing the copper coins
jingling in his hand
I know a difficult calm.

The children on their way to school
turning so effortlessly
down the sloping ridge path,
curving like the slender line
of a winter day's orchid:
thinking "Go safely, fare well,"
I know a sense of peace.

Their hearts, what
are the hearts of these children like?
Small, cold, and mute?
Are they warm as a cousin's silk trousers?
Or like a fireplace
where someone, risen so early in the morning
kindles the fire for someone else?
—Musing, I recall

the line from an old, old song:
"A heart full of healing."

Whatever else they may be,
let your hearts, children, be full
of healing, and all of you
well. May this prayer for you
find you
well.

[352–53]

72

The Child's Dream

In the child's dream a butterfly
has flown away, leaving sunlight behind.
Waking from that dream laughing,
reaching with eyes and cheeks,
the child tries to grasp the sunlight
falling to the floor
from a hole in the paper window.
If mother could be like her child
this way, life would truly be perfect.

[346]

At a Wine House near Taegu

Some days after
the celebration of my sixtieth *
year, one night I found
a small wine house
near Taegu, where the girl
who came and sat by me
seemed just the age
I had been in grade school.
No more those days to play with
than to eat, but still
the fun we had
tickling the girls!
Lost again in longing
I heard that girl say "Well,
is there anything else you want?"
and suddenly we were tickling under the arms,
soles of our feet, laughing
as I haven't laughed in years.
I left her a new
ten-dollar bill, one
I'd received on my birthday,
and hoped we might
"Meet again soon?"
I found my way back
only a few days later,
but the girl by then
was gone,
bundled up and started
again on some wandering trail.
The old poet can't repeat

* The sixtieth birthday marks the full
cycle of a lifetime.

with another
what happened.
That visit was my last;
no way
back to the repetition.

[370]

Snowy Night

On Cheju Island where I spent
Christmas night my sixtieth year
wandering about
and met that girl in the wine house
by the shore—
she had learned my poem
"Beside a Chrysanthemum"
from her high-school language book
and still could recite it perfectly.
When some pesky drinking friend said
"Here, come meet the writer,"
she drew to my side and hid
her eyes in the folds of my coat,
sobbing—that child:
Is she crying somewhere as the snow falls this night?
Or have her tears dried? Has she learned to laugh out loud?

[372]

In the Rain

Some young man of Silla times
sweating, there in the woods
doing it with some girl,
suddenly drawn to the falling
red persimmon, just goes rolling off—
if I could come to life that suddenly
just once!

Thinking of the drops
of rain in a sudden shower
as medicine, perhaps
somehow they could be
just that.

[375]

Cold Wine

Morning, worn out, exhausted after writing all night,
Managing to go on by wetting my throat with cold wine.
How I long for that lady in the rich man's house
where they paid fifty thousand
      for each sixtieth-birthday verse.
Oh if only a line might form of
      fifteen or sixteen such ladies!

[389]

Heron with One Foot Raised

In Yi Tong-baek's "Song of the Birds"
are the lines:
    "Moon bright   autumn water   cold sand;
    Heron with one foot raised."

If all the world were late autumn's chilly waters,
what point would there be in having both feet cold and wet?

Keep one foot less cold by holding it up;
when the other begins to ache, change over,
raising the foot that grew painful in the water.

Surely there can be no doubt.
Is there another piece of wisdom more complete?

[393]

Like the Moon Going Westward   (1980)

Nevada

Even if there were
such a thing as a mouse
that could live
without eating
a thing

how could there be snakes
that could live on
such mice?

Ah, this place
formed in barren, vast
desolation,
where nothing
at all should live:
Nevada!
Nevada!

[396]

Mother and Child
on Ottawa's Twenty-Mile Rink

Ottawa, coldest capital under the skies:
today with the temperature rising
to twenty-five below, the weather
suits these Canadians for skating.

Where the men and women skaters
fly like swallows just touching the waters,
passing like the gentle east wind
across the hard-frozen river's twenty-mile rink,
a young mother, still green at the ear,
and right behind, sturdily following,
goes her two- or three-year-old child.

Hatched that one child
not far away nor long ago, somewhere,
somehow gave that child the instruction
necessary to be brought along
bundled tight in the sled just behind:
now she glides by as if she were bound
for home somewhere in the skies.
Like our faery of long ago
who boiled up a stew of mugwort
to leave her unlucky man;
like the swan
girl
who grew wings once again
and flew off with her only child,
she flies along now so swiftly.

[420]

84

Come to Mexico

The snake
and the tiger
grappled and fought.
The snake
winning
became the sun,
and the tiger
losing, the moon
for this land.

This quite mysterious
land.
Settling in
to live
in Mexico,
one covers up in daytime
and at night sets forth
the tiger's meal.

Listen,
for us
there are no snakes or tigers in store,
just vomiting suddenly all the blood I'd saved,
off to the hospital, getting filled up again
with blood borrowed from Mexicans,
and then waiting for the day
my psychological condition
should improve.

[425]

The Hippy Market in Sao Paulo

From the cheapest cowhide in Brazil
the cheapest Korean in Brazil
manufactures in all of Brazil
the most beautiful bags.
Wearing very dark glasses,
whether for the tears or something more,
sits in Sao Paulo's hippy market, selling . . .
And one old wanderer in this world of scribblers,
I bought that too, putting it over my shoulder,
on the long road again setting off . . .

[446]

Kilimanjaro Sunrise

At sunrise
on Kilimanjaro
what is it the three peaks
                    —grandfather,
                                father,
                        and son—
in silent communication
agree to do?

By a tree of dawn
just the height of a giraffe
they reveal a giraffe couple
as they tear off and eat the leaves.
They reveal a kiss as the couple recalls
love, a kiss just as still
as still can be.

[450]

Ajame

The capital of the coastal land of elephant tusks,
Abidjan, where my black friend Ajame
has neither doorplate nor home address,
family tree, nor age.

When I asked "How old are you?"
pointing at the tree in his yard
he said "Born the same year
as that thing, I was,
but I've forgotten just when.
I've forgotten when.
But what do you want to make
of reckoning up the years that way anyhow?"
He answered so, and laughed
gik gik gik gik, gik gik gik
with the sound of a grasshopper chirring.

I was sorry I asked,
very very sorry indeed.
Laughing madly with that *gik gik gik,*
like a grasshopper just out in the sun
dancing a real go-go dance,
with the words to the song soaking from his body,
his sweat:
      "What will you do, what will you do,
      with a thing like that, your age?
      What will you make, what will you make,
      of such a thing as a family tree?"

[459]

Genial Toledo

Poor and hungry people, souls,
ghosts too, starved as Tu Fu,
should gather at least once
in Toledo.
All who want beefsteak cheap,
and to their heart's content,
Toledo is the place to go.
For lean calf;
double the portions of other places
but the price is the same in Toledo.
The Emperor, it is said,
Hirohito himself praised the taste.
So it happened
that once upon a time
a starving painter
El Greco drifted here,
put on weight and turned out
paintings worth a look.
Highly acclaimed, in Western
eyes . . .

[465]

Song of Paris

Tastier and less pretentious
than scorched rice at the bottom of a pot
in a temple on Buddha's birthday;
longer and plumper than a pretty girl's arms,
Parisian bread is just two hundred *won*
for a loaf that leaves a portion to save
after three meals in a day.

    Weary traveler, penniless scholar,
    won't you come some time to Paris to live?

Butter and sausage, ham and milk
are sold inexpensively still;
a room that costs two hundred a month
is fit for a lord to inhabit.
And if you become a man of sincerity
a lovely woman will find you.

    Weary traveler, penniless scholar,
    won't you come some time to Paris to live?

On the road to Flower Marble Village
dog dung lies here and there
because people's hearts are generous,
not given to stinginess even in dreams.
Like the fragrances that drift through Maroni,
the Parisians and Parisiennes pass by laughing.

    Weary traveler, penniless scholar,
    won't you come some time to Paris to live?

When dusk reaches the alleyways of Paris
cheerful wine tables appear on the streets.
Traveler with just five hundred left in your pocket,
spend it for the biggest jug of beer you can find.
When she sees, a lovely woman will draw near,
clap her hands and tell you "Well done!" with no pretense.

> Weary traveler, penniless scholar,
> won't you come some time to Paris to live?

[470–71]

Mont Blanc: A Story

Once in the winter there came a bride and a groom to Mont Blanc for their honeymoon. On a cliff the groom misstepped and fell, went down and no matter how they looked, no matter where they searched they did not find him. And there are those who say it was the work of the mountain goddess, covetous of the groom . . .

Though a year came and went, searching and searching discovered no trace of the groom, not a suggestion of his shape in the rocks, the earth, the streams. And so the bride had no choice but to live there in the village, in a straw-thatched cottage, waiting and searching until one year, then two had passed; then three, five, ten, and many times ten years had passed, and the bride was an old woman with hair the color of scallion root.

Then it happened, early one spring as the snow was melting in the mountain village. By the side of a mountain stream the bride at last saw her groom again as he floated down in the water, and though years had passed since his death, his face, hair, and skin possessed the same youthfulness of the newly married.

Some say that on the other face of the mountain, frozen solid and covered with snow the year round, the groom fell, was caught between rocks and held in the ice for many tens of years, until that one warm spring day when all was melted and floated down. So they say, while others say "No." In the story they tell, it was the goddess.

[477]

Dawn Impression of Zürich

Sunrise still far off.
The white and the pink marronnier,
and the wild roses as well
are all still drowsy;
but the most diligent
bird in all of Switzerland,
the amsel, in flocks of hundreds and hundreds
all fluttering and hopping about,
chattering *gil–gil–gil* . . .
gil–gil–gil . . .
acting just as frivolous as frivolous
can be, tickling the arms and legs,
the ears and armpits of all of us
who would go on sleeping
with their showers of laughter.
Like orioles, magpies, and a flock
of chattering sixteen-year-old girls,
as the hundreds and thousands of amsels
pour down their tickling, noisy laughter,
even a general could not ignore it.
You have heard no doubt
how the people of Zürich work their fingers
to the bone, never resting
still as a lotus, as a lion,
and how well they live,
stomachs full with the fruits of their labors?
I cannot help thinking
—just my foolish opinion—
their success is due
to the lovely tickling
of thousands of amsels at dawn.

[478]

Swiss Shepherd Horn

The sound of that horn purchased in the pasture lands by the side of a lake in Switzerland is so very peaceful, instead of the buzzer for calling people to my room I am now using this horn.

When I blow the double blast from my room, a sixty-year-old granny—my wife—is always first to hear it, before anyone else in the house. Answering "Yes?" like a primary-school student girl she hurries along; and when I look up at her face, her expression has somehow become child-like again.

Is it any wonder that when I think of all those things brought back from East and West, what most appeals to me now is this Swiss shepherd boy's horn?

[481]

Swiss Cock-a-Doodle-Do Watch

Eyes set to a goddess of the Alps,
mouth to a faery of the Jungfrau;
bathed together with a Rhine mermaid,
grew tired of kingship and serfdom both
and left them to live with the sun and moon light;
a watch manufactured with total precision:
Traveler, if a bit of your journey money remains,
why not part with two hundred dollars
and take one of these away with you?

I liked the Geneva watch-seller's story so much,
from watches clustered like crickets in a bush
I selected one and tucked it in my pocket,
a watch that sounded the hours
with a rooster's "cock-a-doodle-do!"

He has already passed on to the next world,
but Professor Yang Chu-dong would have said "Not bad."
Professor Yang, trusting only that old watch as it
sounded the hourly "ting-a-ling" from his vest; living on
skimpy fees by the numbers of lectures, worried the next would
    be late,
trusting implicitly the "ting-a-ling" in his pocket,
Professor Yang is the one who might have said
"Not a bad watch at all."

[479]

Vienna

The middle-aged gentlemen of Vienna
still wear soft felt hats.
Bending at the waist they perform
salutations quite nicely.
When bringing a Korean home,
a Korean like me,
they unfurl our country's flag
and display it properly.
They may even trust their own wives.

Should one run a bit short of money
dining in the restaurants of Vienna,
the discount is easily arranged.
Certainly, certainly. And the combs in Vienna
won't injure the head;
their teeth are round.

The waters of what is called
the Blue Danube
are rather nasty to see.
With cello accompaniment,
the song makes it all blue again
with a lie surely prettier than truth.

Even Beethoven, a musician
of the most delicate
nerves, felt so much at home
in this unpretentious place,
he stays on; his tomb
remains in this foreign land.

[482]

Cologne Cathedral

Standing in front of Cologne Cathedral, epitome of Gothic architecture, I heard the following conversation between earth and sky, the kind of conversation that amuses a traveler like me from the East.

The Cathedral:
O Lord, look down! Vouchsafe to look!
Is there another's love more fervent, prayers or
faith that have soared more loftily than these?
Piercing the fiery holes in the sky, the burning
ascension of pointedness!
And bathed, washed in the lovely fragrance
of Cologne's waters, finest in the world,
cleaner even than the stars that would cleave
so close to you—See, please see!—
These pointed towers that burning stand
like the tallest forest: Even the stones
that sleep lying down, we make stand,
lighted with fire!

And God replies:

Devotion so heated, so impatient
is most commendable but so exceedingly,
such soarings upward as you result in such pointedness,
or to speak frankly even we
find it difficult at times to endure
such heated and painful devotion.
Life discovers levels, inevitably, of attitude
as a pup that rests by the fire,
or the crowd in a demonstration
that in its noisesome coming and going
does reach the heavens,

which in my heart I do not favor.
Might you live round?
Or rather low and round, humbly
rounded, do you think?
In that event I might note
that your modesty would not be cause
for overlooking you.

[483–84]

The Floor in Goethe's House

For how many hundreds of years,
how many thousands of times
have generations of women worn
their hands down
                    polishing
and polishing the wide boards of this floor?

Mark of the hands of so many generations
of good-hearted people;
clear mirror that deepens with each generation;
and the sky joined in kindly understanding—
where they seem joined in wearing away together,

rest in their warm embrace.
That floor gleaming in Goethe's house
promises comfort, and recovery from any illness,
whatever its cause.

Fruit of the mulberry tree
and ball of the cotton plant
show their faces in this floor,
reflecting as if new born.

How utterly colorless it would all appear
if one Goethe at least had not been born
in a corner so well tended as this.

[485]

Moonlight and the Mermaid

Where the sea was more powerful
than heavens or earth,
the prince's love proved weaker
than the mermaid's.
On a moonlit night
as the prince faded tendrilly away,
alone by the shore
the mermaid came out and sat
curving, thinking of him.
The light of the moon as well,
helplessly washing, washing, washing down,
was dyed the color of the sea,
only the color of the sea.

[496]

Michelangelo's Pieta

Michelangelo!
Immortal spirit neither aging nor dying,
you who understood how one lives in youthfulness,
how truly praiseworthy you are!

A young woman's face, Mary
the mother who holds her son's body
brought down from the cross where it was nailed:
Michelangelo,
you had such keen vision!

Michelangelo, you fashioned
the corpse of our Lord Jesus Christ
as if he had just returned home
from a long journey, and after drowsing
and dreaming a brief dream,
had stretched out in deepest slumber.
You are one who knew well
that immortality of the East.

Knowing you had not read the Buddhist scriptures
nor the Taoist canon, I affirm
your truly prodigious gifts.
Well might you have lived a long life
in our land, robed in jade green
of the Taoist immortals.

[512]

Nymphs, Bonfires, and the Groves of Rome

When night enters the woody groves near Rome,
bonfires of the nymphs from long ago
can be seen even now, here and there.

And if you fancy yourself a satyr,
attach a goat's tail
and go out to prowl, seeking those fires,
when you stop, warming your cupped hands,
like being that comes from nothingness,
calling in her pretty voice "Oh my!"
one nymph does approach you.

And yet those nymphs of the Roman groves
are stained with the capitalism of beggars;
they ask, for this, many tens of dollars in fees.

Fellow, satyr; satyrish fellow:
If perchance like the satyrs of old
you managed to bring a reed flute,
it could only suit the elegy you will play.

[519]

By a Bridge on the Arno

Where clear-complexioned men and women,
free of medieval ecclesiastics,
now in paintings fill the houses
they once inhabited

in Florence, origin
of the Renaissance,

passing the marble-paved alleyways
and over a bridge on the Arno,
I see a road leading far, far away.

At this place by the bridge-end, our poet Dante
would meet his eternal love, Beatrice.
To add another round to their story of love
seems a miraculous occasion.

Beauty gathered in freedom,
flesh touching, the feast enjoyed
to the fullest.
                    These too make the breath
run short.

By this alleyway, like a road
stretching endlessly into woods grown thick
in the distance:
                    Dante and Beatrice,
their endless tale of love
found in the appropriate place.

[519]

By the Ionian Sea

PLAYING A REED FLUTE PURCHASED IN CORINTH

Do this, the beast–god Pan said, who stood
stark naked in the trees' dense shade

with three cows
                              playing the flute.

So in the market at Corinth I bought one,
went to the edge of the Ionian Sea,
stood there and played it.

Rough Poseidon, God of the Sea,
recognized that sound.
Rising from the waves he whispered these words:

"Truly my life has become very different;
I spend much of it just playing a thing like that."

"If you want to listen, come follow me,"
he continued.
                              So I
did, plunging in over my head,
then using the frog crawl I had learned as a child.

Although the tune was a bit different
from the tune on land, the flute's tone
without question was the same.

Of many things that ancient Greece made,
this remains quite thoroughly alive,
penetrating the depths of the Ionian Sea.

[523]

Greetings from the Village of Nazareth

In the place where young Jesus,
his father Joseph, the carpenter,
and mother Mary once lived all together,
I said "Stay well" as a parting salutation.
A grandfatherly guide corrected that expression.
"What is it for me to stay here alone?
I shall go with you, together in your heart."

[525]

At the Wailing Wall

People of a land
   lost,
     no matter how cruelly,
let them stand
   wailing,
     pounding their fists
against the hard wall
    for a thousand years,
for two thousand,
   three:
     then they will realize
that fearsome independence.

Let them stand in lamentation with the great spirits
of Jesus, Jeremiah; let them beat on the wall
with their fists for three thousand years.
Then will that wholly awesome independence be known.

The wall of Jeremiah,
who seeing his land destroyed by Babylon
beat his breast and wailed in lamentation;
wall of Jesus' lamentation,
who saw his land destroyed by Rome
and vowed as a spirit to return and conquer;
of the Israelites, all but a few
driven from that wall and forced
to wander helpless through the world.
Now after an interval of precisely one thousand,
eight hundred years
    they gather together,
again joining in bands, one and two, and many.
Back again, they pound with their fists on the wall,

standing in affirmation of the vow
to revive, to reestablish their land.

Israel! Symbol of a nation's undying soul!

Only the hair beneath the ear of tears
grows thick; only a luckless people
who have lost their land;
with the hair beneath sorrow's ear
braided, they stand, swearing an oath to heaven:
for one thousand years, for two thousand, three,
beating on the wall, wailing
for that most severe independence,
that we shall know its coming.

[528–29]

Wisdom of the Turkish Gentleman

Where tourists wait for taxis
on the streets of Istanbul
the Turkish gentleman appears, fluent
in English and French,
with a fine mustache.
He asks the destination:
"What direction might you be taking?"
And if by good fortune
your destinations are the same,
striking a genteel bargain he comes along,
saying "I will be able to cut the fare
in half; no trouble. So
let us travel together a while."
Thus he goes about for nothing,
stroking his mustache,
never failing to arrange the discount
of fifty percent for a taxi fare
that would cost a tourist double.

[530]

Egypt's Maid

Egyptian maid
dressed in a swimsuit—
a candidate, surely, for Miss Universe—
wearing a rainbow-colored one-piece
mini-suit, she adds gold bells
to her gold anklets.

She steps then with distant pride
more like the bedroom at midnight
or the stars, the sun and moon.

In one hand she holds folded a duck's wing,
and each time that duck's wing flutters,
that girl's flesh trembles too.

[535]

Map of the Arabian Desert

Fiery sands
where the straight sword bends into a scimitar;
where love and wine, compassion and forgiveness
are punished. Ah, the endless desert
heat that boiled the eye,
boils the eye.

This madness—Where is it from?
A man and a woman discovered in secret love
buried in sand to their necks:
their dying cries as stones batter their heads
sound the gravely injured flower's cry.

A beggar's scream, most wretched of beggars
forced to steal; that beggar's scream
as the blade severs hand from wrist
is burnt up, the next flower's cry,
in the blazing heavens.

And the fortunate ones, blessed
with Allah's special dispensation,
lie down for a rest
by the oasis, or in a private room
by the Red Sea, embracing four wives.
As they wash away the sweat
of that heavy labor,
again they assume
their deceitful smiles.

[536]

Kalpa Time

On the people of Nepal, Sakyamuni's * birthplace,
who wash their bodies with the waters of Himalayan valleys
and almost never use soap to bathe,
the fine dust gathers through time
deep as the mountain's shadow.

If one is to take and live the span
of five million, three hundred and twenty thousand years
as if it were a day,
this
happening so naturally
is surely as it should be.

[541]

* Sakyamuni, another name for Buddha,
was born in Nepal. He was said to have
been poisoned in the manner described
in the next poem.

Everest's Highest Peak Says

You whose love is so very deep and big!
Even if someone has fed you poison,
as you know the pain, vomiting blood
and about to die, until the very last breath
has left your body,
                                    for the poison
in the mind of the assassin to dissolve
in the plentifulness of your love,
and with his mind appeased then to receive
you and go on, steadily
you must speak with him,
persuading him.
For the man Sakyamuni,
born in this valley two thousand,
five hundred years ago,
there was no other way
then reasoning and persuasion,
no other way at all.

[542]

Song of the Indian Wanderers

A house? Do you ask of a house?
On days when it rains for the sadness of heaven,
just stop beneath the roof of a temple.
What would it mean to have a house to one's self?

Clothes, then? Do you ask about clothes?
The clothes of heaven don't need stitching, they say;
the sari that wraps the body round like a cloud
is all that is needed to wear.

Food? Do you ask about food?
Only when hunger surpasses the feeding
does the mind become crisp and clear.
One spoonful to eat! Ten spoonfuls of hunger!

And life? Do you ask now of life?
To flow in harmony always with heaven,
like the Ganges never going dry:
the sons and the daughters flowing on, flowing on.

[546]

Woman of India

Do not ask an Indian woman
what time it is. Just ask
is it day or night.
Do not ask by any account
whether this is today,
yesterday, or tomorrow.

Ask carefully, in full detail,
the flower well hidden in the night,
the flower blooming
visibly in the day.
That is the only thing;
it will be whispered
in full detail.

If asked "What is your price?"
they do not seem to know at all.
Plus infinity
minus infinity
seem like sums
to be reckoned on the fingers.

And suppose some dissolute foreigner
asked an Indian prostitute
"How much shall I give you?"
Why, she wouldn't know at all
what the number might be.

[547]

The Jain Temple in Rainy Calcutta

The Jain goddess in rainy Calcutta
begins with the early-evening drinking hour
to float a blood-red crescent moon between her brows,
her high-set eyes the thin color of dark waters.
She holds the jade flute in her lovely hands,
playing it so entrancingly, a peacock lifts in flight
to that melody—
              And Oh, Oh, what should one do?
Take the light silk coverlet, the one dyed
with juice of the mock-orange blossom;
wrap it round, wrap it round, and briefly nap.
Oh, Oh, just drift off to sleep.

And so at last on a rainy evening in Calcutta,
the priests of the Jain temple
close the main gate and go drifting
into the soft rumble of their snores

till someone is suddenly banging on the gate,
a traveler arriving at the temple.
Disconcertedly rubbing their eyes
the priests hold out something,
saying "Buy just one"—a picture
of the slightly tipsy goddess.

[548]

Elephants of Thailand

The elephants of Thailand perform their bows extremely well.
To their mothers and fathers, of course;
and also to their offspring they bow
very well indeed.
                    Familiar living creatures,
of course; and to living creatures
not so familiar, they perform their deep bows.
To anything that can be seen
as well as what might very well
never be seen they perform
their deep formal bows without fail.
They enjoy in the gap
between time and distance
their relatively uneventful independence.

[552]

The Pedlar Women of Wu-Lai

The Kaosha pedlar women of Wu-Lai
loan their handsome umbrellas free of charge
to the tourists on rainy days.
"Take this with you, have a look around,
and then drop it off on your way out."

But one doesn't feel right,
just giving it back on the way out.
As you hand over the coins for an item
or two, they say "Stay just a night at the inn
down there. If you do (coyly laughing)
I'll come find you, I will."

And so as you wait at the inn
down there, swallowing saliva as the night
draws on, she is there, showing you this
and showing you that from a big pack
all wrapped up, and she says
"Buy one, why don't you? Just one is all."

So without much choice in the matter,
as you are about to buy one of this
and two of that, and more, one by one
she picks up what is left, carefully
placing them back in the sack. Then at last,
scampering off like a mountain weasel
she calls "Thank you, now. And sleep well,
won't you?"

[554]

China's Free Verse Poet

Chou Meng-tieh, poet of freedom.
Day after day, in the shade
of some roadside trees in a corner
of Taipei he opens up ten
or so books of poems.
Browsing through this one
or that, he submerges
in meditation.
Seated this way
if one book is sold,
then with the price of one book,
and if two books are sold
during the long, long day
then with the price of two books:
he uses that money for something to eat
and a place to sleep.
Spends it for a place
in the common dormitory room
of a cheap inn.
With no way to repay
another's invitation,
he puts in no attendances,
and though no one knows
when, nor in what mountain valley
he cleans them, his cotton robes
are always clean.
His grip is so strong
shaking hands can be painful,
and his glance is that strong too.
When in my roundabout way
I asked whether he might find
some woman to love and have children with,

he just laughed with his strong, white teeth
and said "As for me, I could,
but would anyone come along
who would say it doesn't hurt?"

[555]

Todaiji

At the Buddhist temple, Todaiji in Nara,
looking carefully at the roof ends, thinking
"Overdone is worse than unfinished,"
or "Climb a pole and play in a red skirt."
These are the sayings that come to mind.

The biggest tile-roof building beneath the skies, Todaiji.
With the curving line of a wing
that would fly away this moment,
like the nose of our Korean bootlet,
just like the tiled rooves of Korea . . .
But then such foolishness, to think
of adding something more to such beauty.

There, on that elegant peak,
two horns of pure gold:
what possible use
is that careless ornamentation?

Battered by a golden horn
like some samurai warrior's cap,
how can one soar with a mind at peace,
and to what sky,
to what inner sphere?

[556]

In the Osaka Station Restroom

Where the sun doesn't shine, in the stinking restroom in Osaka Station, right by the toilets was a thin, long-haired youthful genius type spinning round and round, lost in a solitary disco dance. For him there was only the dance; nothing else seen, thought, or felt as he shifted his feet back and forth and swiveled his body round, shaking with such total concentration.

Call it pitiful; pitiful it was. Or call it laughable; it was that too. But nowhere else in human society has such a thing been seen, such total self-absorption in such a place as this. And somehow it seemed to be a most important aspect of the true and fundamental nature of Japan.

[560]

Other Works in the Columbia Asian Studies Series

NEO-CONFUCIAN STUDIES

Other Works in Asian Studies Series

The Message of the Mind in Neo-Confucian Thought by Wm. Theodore de Bary   1989

MODERN ASIAN LITERATURE SERIES

Modern Japanese Drama: An Anthology, ed. and tr. Ted T. Takaya. Also in paperback ed.   1979
Mask and Sword: Two Plays for the Contemporary Japanese Theater, Yamazaki Masakazu, tr. J. Thomas Rimer   1980
Yokomitsu Rüchi, Modernist, Dennis Keene   1980
Nepali Visions, Nepali Dreams: The Poetry of Laxmiprasad Devkota, tr. David Rubin   1980
Literature of the Hundred Flowers, vol. 1: *Criticism and Polemics,* ed. Hualing Nieh   1981
Literature of the Hundred Flowers, vol. 2: *Poetry and Fiction,* ed. Hualing Nieh   1981
Modern Chinese Stories and Novellas, 1919–1949, ed. Joseph S. M. Lau, C. T. Hsia, and Leo Ou-fan Lee. Also in paperback ed.   1984
A View by the Sea, by Yasuoka Shōtarō, tr. Kären Wigen Lewis   1984
Other Worlds; Arishima Takeo and the Bounds of Modern Japanese Fiction, by Paul Anderer   1984

TRANSLATIONS FROM THE ORIENTAL CLASSICS

Major Plays of Chikamatsu, tr. Donald Keene   1961
Four Major Plays of Chikamatsu, tr. Donald Keene. Paperback text edition   1961
Records of the Grand Historian of China, translated from the *Shih chi* of Ssu-ma Ch'ien, tr. Burton Watson, 2 vols.   1961
Instructions for Practical Living and Other Neo-Confucian Writings by Wang Yang-ming, tr. Wing-tsit Chan   1963
Chuang Tzu: Basic Writings, tr. Burton Watson, paperback ed. only   1964
The Mahābhārata, tr. Chakravarthi V. Narasimhan. Also in paperback ed.   1965
The Manyōshū, Nippon Gakujutsu Shinkōkai edition   1965

Su Tung-p'o: Selections from a Sung Dynasty Poet, tr. Burton Watson. Also in paperback ed.   1965

Bhartrihari: Poems, tr. Barbara Stoler Miller. Also in paperback ed.   1967

Basic Writings of Mo Tzu, Hsün Tzu, and Han Fei Tzu, tr. Burton Watson. Also in separate paperback eds.   1967

The Awakening of Faith, Attributed to Aśvaghosha, tr. Yoshito S. Hakeda. Also in paperback ed.   1967

Reflections on Things at Hand: The Neo-Confucian Anthology, comp. Chu Hsi and Lü Tsu-ch'ien, tr. Wing-tsit Chan   1967

The Platform Sutra of the Sixth Patriarch, tr. Philip B. Yampolsky. Also in paperback ed.   1967

Essays in Idleness: The Tsurezuregusa of Kenkō, tr. Donald Keene. Also in paperback ed.   1967

The Pillow Book of Sei Shōnagon, tr. Ivan Morris, 2 vols.   1967

Two Plays of Ancient India: The Little Clay Cart and the Minister's Seal, tr. J. A. B. van Buitenen   1968

The Complete Works of Chuang Tzu, tr. Burton Watson   1968

The Romance of the Western Chamber (Hsi Hsiang chi), tr. S. I. Hsiung. Also in paperback ed.   1968

The Manyōshū, Nippon Gakujutsu Shinkōkai edition. Paperback text edition.   1969

Records of the Historian: Chapters from the Shih chi of Ssu-ma Ch'ien. Paperback text edition, tr. Burton Watson.   1969

Cold Mountain: 100 Poems by the T'ang Poet Han-shan, tr. Burton Watson. Also in paperback ed.   1970

Twenty Plays of the Nō Theatre, ed. Donald Keene. Also in paperback ed.   1970

Chushingura: The Treasury of Loyal Retainers, tr. Donald Keene. Also in paperback ed.   1971

The Zen Master Hakuin: Selected Writings, tr. Philip B. Yampolsky   1971

Chinese Rhyme-Prose: Poems in the Fu Form from the Han and Six Dynasties Periods, tr. Burton Watson. Also in paperback ed.   1971

Kūkai: Major Works, tr. Yoshito S. Hakeda. Also in paperback ed.   1972

The Old Man Who Does as He Pleases: Selections from the Poetry and Prose of Lu Yu, tr. Burton Watson   1973

Other Works in Asian Studies Series

The Lion's Roar of Queen Śrīmālā, tr. Alex & Hideko
   Wayman   1974
*Courtier and Commoner in Ancient China: Selections from
   the History of the Former Han by Pan Ku,* tr. Burton
   Watson. Also in paperback ed.   1974
Japanese Literature in Chinese, vol. 1: *Poetry and Prose in
   Chinese by Japanese Writers of the Early Period,* tr. Bur-
   ton Watson   1975
Japanese Literature in Chinese, vol. 2: *Poetry and Prose in
   Chinese by Japanese Writers of the Later Peiod,* tr. Bur-
   ton Watson   1976
Scripture of the Lotus Blossom of the Fine Dharma, tr.
   Leon Hurvitz. Also in paperback ed.   1976
Love Song of the Dark Lord: Jayadeva's Gītagovinda, tr.
   Barbara Stoler Miller. Also in paperback ed. Cloth ed.
   includes critical text of the Sanskrit.   1977
Ryōkan: Zen Monk-Poet of Japan, tr. Burton Watson   1977
*Calming the Mind and Discerning the Real: From the Lam
   rim chen mo of Tson-kha-pa,* tr. Alex Wayman   1978
*The Hermit and the Love-Thief: Sanskirt Poems of Bhartri-
   hari and Bilhana,* tr. Barbara Stoler Miller   1978
The Lute: Kao Ming's p'i-p'a chi, tr. Jean Mulligan. Also in
   paperback ed.   1980
*A Chronicle of Gods and Sovereigns: Jinnō Shōtōki of Ki-
   tabatake Chikafusa,* tr. H. Paul Varley   1980
Among the Flowers: The Hua-chien chi, tr. Lois Fusek   1982
Grass Hill: Poems and Prose by the Japanese Monk Gensei,
   tr. Burton Watson   1983
*Doctors, Diviners, and Magicians of Ancient China: Bio-
   graphies of Fang-shih,* tr. Kenneth J. DeWoskin. Also in
   paperback ed.   1983
Theatre of Memory: The Plays of Kālidāsa, ed. Barbara
   Stoler Miller. Also in paperback ed.   1984
*The Columbia Book of Chinese Poetry: From Early Times
   to the Thirteenth Century,* ed. and tr. Burton Watson   1984
*Poems of Love and War: From the Eight Anthologies and
   the Ten Songs of Classical Tamil,* tr. A. K. Ramanujan.
   Also in paperback ed.   1985
The Columbia Book of Later Chinese Poetry, ed. and tr.
   Jonathan Chaves   1986

Other Works in Asian Studies Series

STUDIES IN ORIENTAL CULTURE

19. *Expressions of Self in Chinese Literature*, ed. Robert E. Hegel and Richard C. Hessney   1985
20. *Songs for the Bride: Women's Voices and Wedding Rites of Rural India*, by W. G. Archer, ed. Barbara Stoler Miller and Mildred Archer   1985
21. *A Heritage of Kings: One Man's Monarchy in the Confucian World*, by JaHyun Kim Haboush   1988

COMPANIONS TO ASIAN STUDIES

Approaches to the Oriental Classics, ed. Wm. Theodore de Bary   1959
Early Chinese Literature, by Burton Watson. Also in paperback ed.   1962
Approaches to Asian Civilizations, ed. Wm. Theodore de Bary and Ainslie T. Embree   1964
The Classic Chinese Novel: A Critical Introduction, by C. T. Hsia. Also in paperback ed.   1968
Chinese Lyricism: Shih Poetry from the Second to the Twelfth Century, tr. Burton Watson. Also in paperback ed.   1971
A Syllabus of Indian Civilization, by Leonard A. Gordon and Barbara Stoler Miller   1971
Twentieth-Century Chinese Stories, ed. C. T. Hsia and Joseph S. M. Lau. Also in paperback ed.   1971
A Syllabus of Chinese Civilization, by J. Mason Gentzler, 2d ed.   1972
A Syllabus of Japanese Civilization, by H. Paul Varley, 2d ed.   1972
An Introduction to Chinese Civilization, ed. John Meskill, with the assistance of J. Mason Gentzler   1973
An Introduction to Japanese Civilization, ed. Arthur E. Tiedemann   1974
Ukifune: Love in the Tale of Genji, ed. Andrew Pekarik   1982
A Guide to Oriental Classics, ed. Wm. Theodore de Bary and Ainslie T. Embree, third edition ed. Amy Vladek Heinrich   1989

INTRODUCTION TO ORIENTAL CIVILIZATIONS
Wm. Theodore de Bary, Editor

Sources of Japanese Tradition 1958 Paperback ed., 2 vols.,
  1964
Sources of Indian Tradition 1958 Paperback ed., 2 vols.,
  1964 Second edition 1988, 2 vols.
Sources of Chinese Tradition 1960 Paperback ed., 2 vols., 1964